The Shadow Garden

By

George A. Hart

George A. Hart / Rev. Caesar 999

ISBN: 978-0-9840313-7-5

Notes:

Here is the edited version. I have replaced a few words and very few grammatical mistakes. Some words I originally made up, others I could not decipher. You may replace words with your own or with the words you feel fit best.

The Shadow Garden

Seeing the shadow garden run with your nightmares.
Seeing the shadow garden run with your blood.
Seeing the shadow garden run with your life.
The garden, The garden, The garden.
The shadow garden, The shadow garden, The shadow garden.

Look Garden! Children upon your amidst.
Children in the garden.
Children in the garden.
Shadows lurking in the garden.
Demons and shadows mulching in the garden.
Garden hide your secrets for naughty children might tell.
Garden teach the children and teach them well.
Children in the garden, garden, garden.
Children in the garden, garden, garden.

Children playing games evil games.
Children go home where you lay six feet under where you rot and decay.
Fucking little brats!!
Garden hide your secrets for the naughty children might tell.
Garden teach the children and teach them well.
The shadow garden, garden, garden.
The shadow garden, garden, garden.

Do you know the garden is pure hell?
Children the garden has taught you to fight.
The garden has taught you to destroy.
For children you are immortal.

It is written that a many of mighty youth shall rise.
To fight from the garden they came.
Once there armada is released they shall crush all in their path.
Be ready, for the time will come for your great victory.
So be brave and prepared for that day will soon be here.

The Releasing

Run with your glory.
Run with your fate.
Run with your soul.
Go now, Go now.
Mighty and righteous children of the realm.

Fly with the wind.
Soar across the sky.
Be one with the land.
You are released to do your mighty task.
Go, Go, Go.
This time is yours and meant for yours only.
So go, go, go.
Stake your destiny.
Raise your arms to battle.
Fight like you never fought before.
Go, go, go now.
For this an unholy war.

Sent-on a journey to complete a task never completed by any other war before.
Sent to finish the end.
They started the wheels of time speeding up again.
We must slow the grinder of time once more.
They started something that we're going to finish.
We've been waiting so long to open the gates of the shadow garden.

The Wastelands

Joined by the youth.
The guardians have been forced back past the wastelands.
Back past the hills.
Back past the lakes.
Back to the ends of the earth.

Sprouting wings and being forced off the earth.
Where we can bash the wrath of hell upon them.
Destroy those <u>Fuckers.</u>
No mercy to the makers.
The ones they call the Gods.
Finally we shall be free of soul imprisonment.

Paristal is returned to normal.
Life is ravaged but kept as is.
Destiny lingers mercifully under balance.
Change is hesitating but land sliding to move.
Cause the waste lands are plagued for eternity.
The waters are cursed.
And the hills are covered with death.
But in time the earth shall always return itself to a normal state.

The Arrival

When they arrived it seemed all was well.
Until everyone started dying.
Dieing when they came dying.
Not realizing that every soul enters the shadow garden.
Where you're given your immortality.

We've came a long way since we were made of flesh.
We fought them in space and lost.
We fought them on earth and lost.
Then we fought them in our minds and won.
The gardens full of children.
Children in the garden.
Children in the garden.

They fought to the garden.
And to the mighty.
The sacred.
The mighty and sacred crypt, crypt, crypt.
Where the ancient leader lays immortal.

From the depths of hell led the depraving derelict.
Who deprives us of our immortality's.
But know from the darkness.
The recognition of the revelation has begun.
We're promised immortal immortality from now till then.

The Crypt

The crypt, crypt, crypt.
The mighty crypt, crypt, crypt.
The sacred crypt, crypt, crypt.

Here lies the child of the crypt, crypt, crypt.
Here lies the immortal child of the crypt, crypt, crypt.
Where he awaits the coming of the guardians.
Then he alone shall raise a child army of destruction, destruction, destruction.
Then the gates of the shadow garden shall open.
And one-million-one shall flow from the garden, garden, garden.

The keepers of the garden, garden, garden.
Stalk for prey.
Stalking cops and soldiers and traitors to the realm.
And they give offerings to the crypt, crypt, crypt.
The mighty crypt, crypt, crypt.
The sacred crypt, crypt, crypt.

Child of the crypt teach them and teach them well.
Teach them to fight.
Teach them to destroy.
Teach them to win.

The Sacrifice

Sacrificial sacrifice coming nearer and nearer to you.
Sacrificial sacrifice made under candle light.
Contracts have been written.
Your soul is given.
Beauty-ful child it's not your choice.
You've been chosen for this sacrifice.

Give me power don't take my strength.
Resent destruction tearing resurrection.
Tasting blood of the knife.
Giving the caller ultimate demon powers.
Drinking from the golden goblet.
We see the world at our mercy.
Breath-ed sacrilege of the age.
Sabotaging the dead of the tides.

Death is soothing.
Death is relieving.
Death is for you.

We sacrifice to call the power of evil.
Which shall save us from the guardians of good.
That wish to destroy us.
For we have the power to defeat a many.

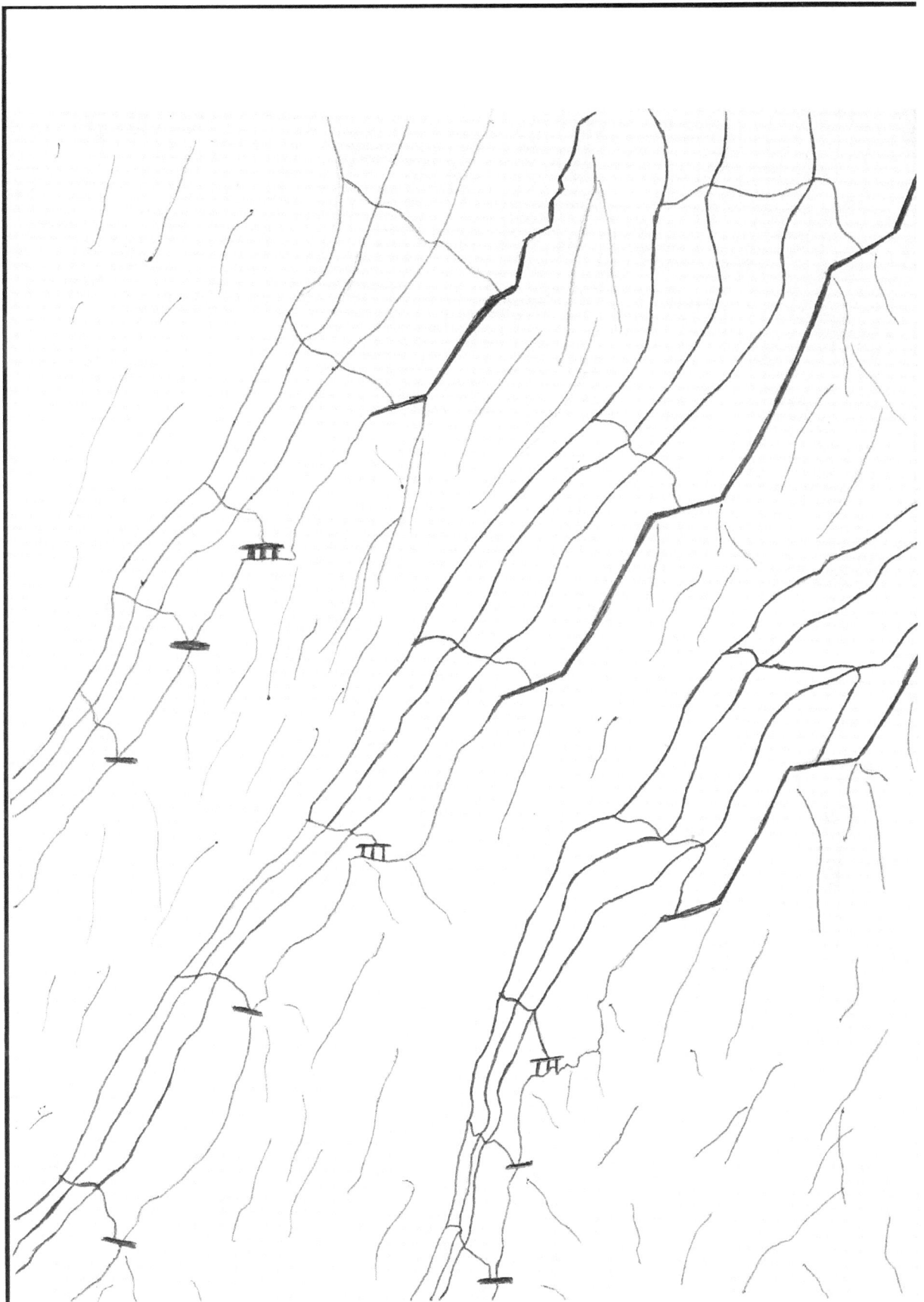

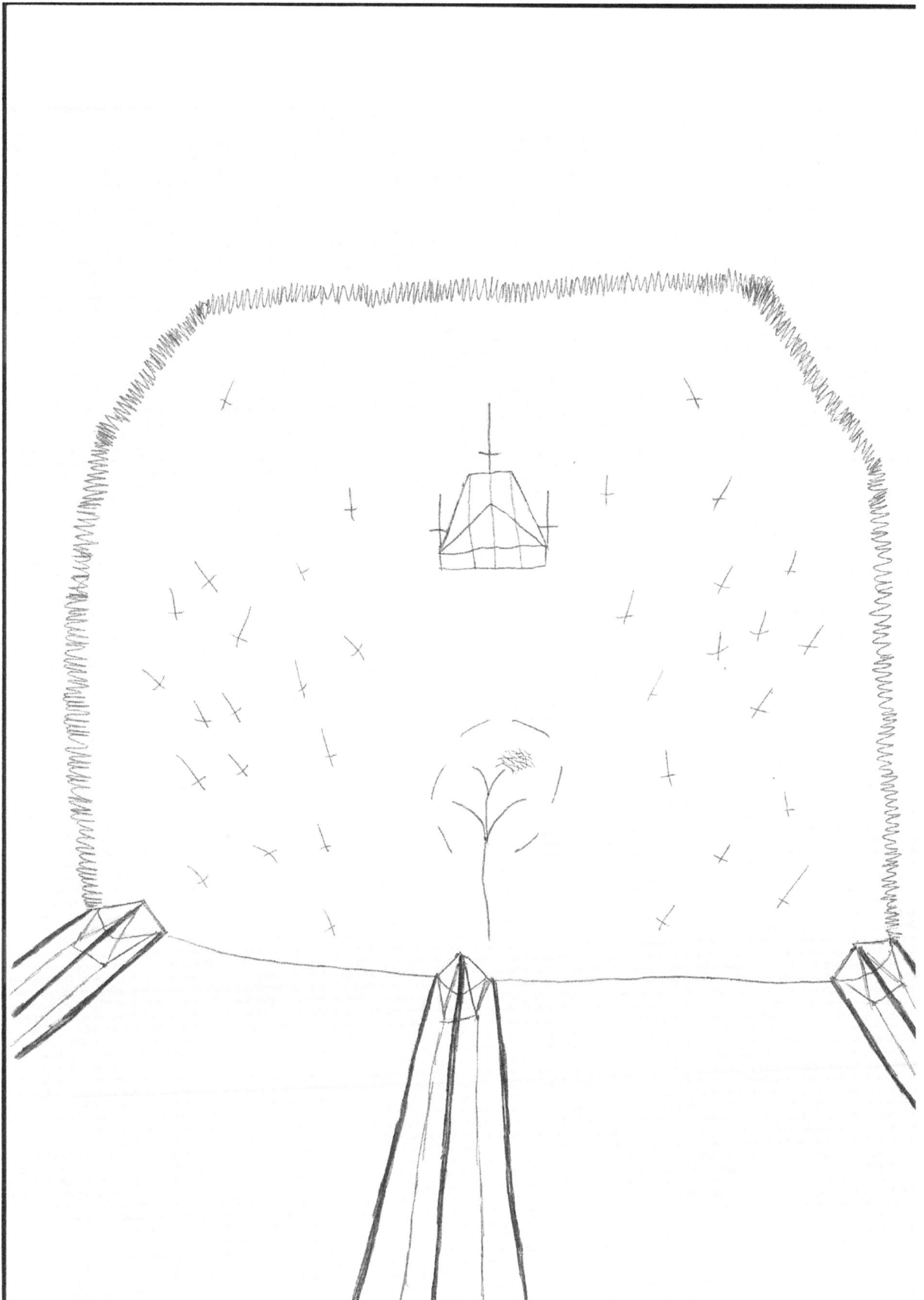

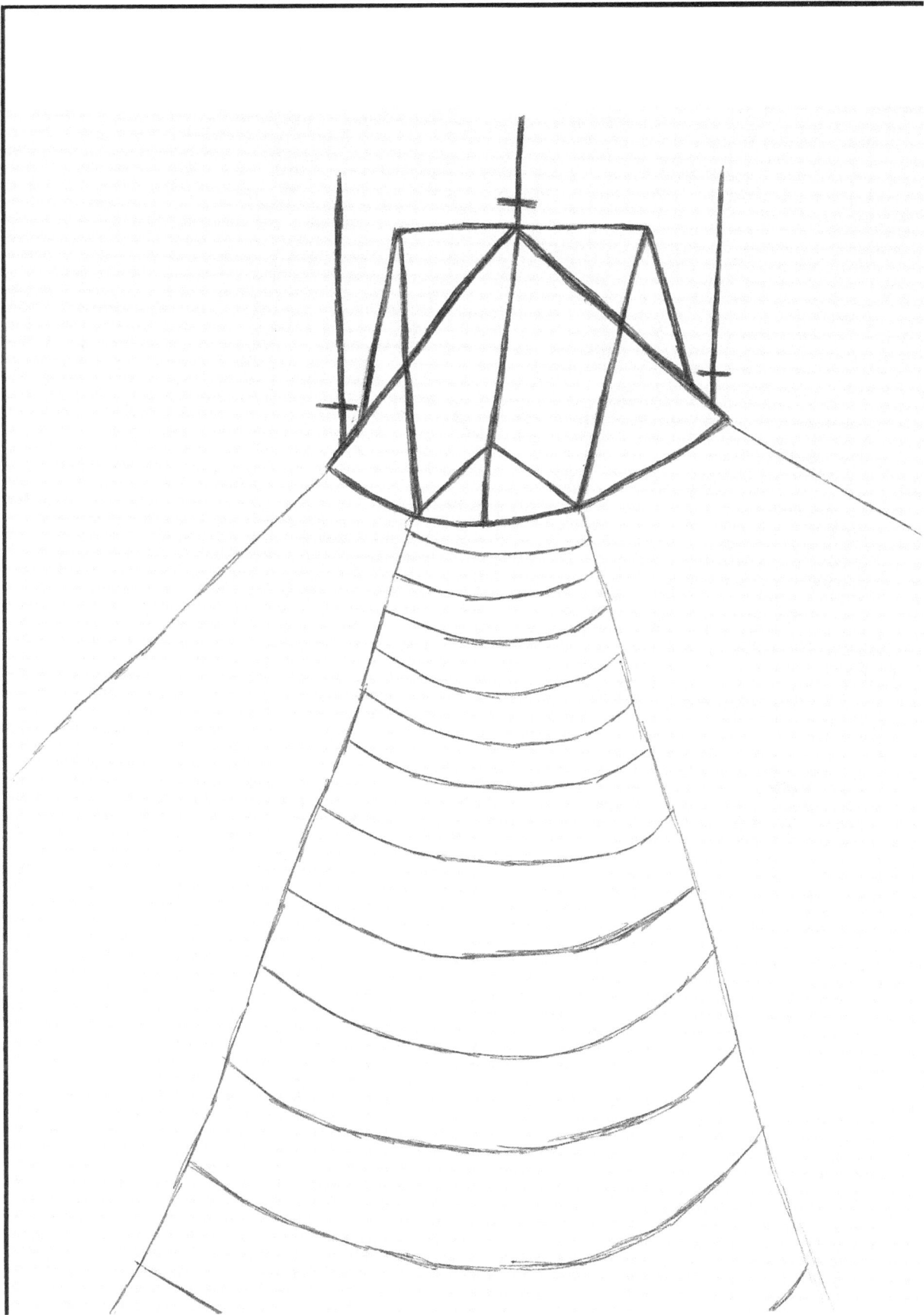

The Incantation To Be

Balad center collapsing under courage.
Seeing the ravaged land.
Cowardly youth marching on.
Marking their trail abiding the law of war they are.
Triggering Destruction.
Ending in despairing laybid dilemma of horridly bearing bilateen.

By passed abrasion.
Sighted for masses bladely domed upon.
Stormed up carriage speckled eye.
Choking life stealing the planet.
Jarred a part it was.
Sending us on an endless Journey.
Through the scape lever of the space and time continual.

Braking for nothing fighting for all.
Gathering clearance to the heavens.
Searching far and wide they did.
Sweeping the realm.
Waking the tarnished beat of cursing chaveses.
Smelling joke late of rhyme.
Sparking confusion through all.
Turned to no one.
Helplessly lost creeping shame.
Never looking back at the perking waste.
Corrupting sting.
Banning Rally.
Wicked stain.

Trekk

Spiny lesser made to call.
Calling children embracing All.
Spanning structure potening sight not to be found.
Germing fleas wrapping you and me.
Waited for slaving tune.
Pondering wasteland to be seen.

Northward bound bragging people of the realm.
Wild waters tempest ocean coast.
Tenting based at the path to solitaire.
Webbing factor shaving stout on hand.

Assembling youth raising power.
Bleeding insanity.
Bubbling Trekk entering timeless sleep into the past.
Judging luxury tablet of the overlord.
Slender wave over thrown.
Jolly lover of precious debut.
Challenging mercy to listen to you.

Whistle bristle.
Don't you see.
We're the mending lat.
Perlicking silent wonders.
To be fastened.

The Once Countdown

Stolen premonition.
Talented speaker Boasting Lateral creation.
Tormenting the battle left behind.
It was said and done with in one Blink of the eye.
Last hope first sight of careless choice.
Once thought as a great apparition.
Jerking deep into the mind.
Turning rapidly about.

Darken light burning at daybreak.
Racing world to the end.
Parking over spacious grave.
Magic tome hovering wide.
For we the prophets have seen the naked end.
Crushing all before the light.

Fortune lost at the term.
Sleek base hidden back through the smoke.
Only survivors bracing the earth.
Meant to be as it was.
Gallanted soldiers walking on.
The new world has risen.
Drastically on the move.
Opening path to the future realm.
Where we shall live in high-archy.
Hondering endless life.
Sharing with no one.
The future has past and the wars are not yet to begin.
For our new world has Begun.

Vegetable Men

Wake up vegetable.
Taking leave of this phantom.
Character of dark lesome.
Speaking man on the prowl.
Blending words chanting all around.

Spinning ball lit a fire.
Burning wildly.
Upper world to be destroyed.
Breaking temple.
Sieging unit held by hand.
Pushing a button releasing our land.
Sealing fate.

Wake up vegetable.
Taking leave of this phantom.
Character of dark lesome.
Speaking man on the prowl.
Blending words chanting all around.

Strangling seed mulching death.
Dirty pile.
Staring blindly across the serpent lane.
Chalid star to be plunged.
Craterly into scope.
Curdling saber crashing down.
Blistering rush.
Cheating game.
Durble krebb.

Mirror of Blind Reflection

Angling reflection made to see.
Branding snake monstrous bait.
Snowing wrath of pollen.
To be broken of heart.
Channeling might to be thrown.
Tanning breakage regularly.
Striking clown thought of phrase.
Raking shallow bottoms.
Under training life spans.
Sending message to be interpreted.

Burning earthly possession.
Staring bravely.
Tracking under thy.
The worthless history.
Rendering caring breasts.
Perfect world under siege.
Shadow of wisdom come to be.
Last effort plainly seen.
Harrow of darkness is changing me.

Draining life.
Whispering to you and me.
Dreaded souls of our people.
Raining blood on the way.
For we've seen into.
The mirror of blind reflection.
Seeing the youth withering away.
Stranded on a lonely isle.
Cast away.
The mirror has broken.
And we're lost here to decay.

I see a lifeboat waited down.
Beyond the horizon.
Comely drifting farther away.
This cold place has no name.
It's just a blind reflection.

Burning earthly possession.
Staring bravely.
Tracking under thy.
The worthless history.
Rendering caring breasts.
Perfect world under siege.
Shadow of wisdom come to be.
Last effort plainly seen.
Harrow of darkness is changing me.

Returning Time

Time is on my hands.
Time it is.
Time of life.
Time of death.
Time to escape.
Time to Flee.
Raging oddity of configuration.
Lust for life being it.
Baring jewels come to take.
Come to harness before size.
Lifting fingers of time.
Sought after which is yours and mine.

Reigning power over all.
Joining laughter in arms.
Pulling time to a halt.
Stopping now.
Stop of life.
Stop of death.
Gradually decaying in the mind.
Bulging, Leaning, seeing the drifting bellows on my hands.
Delightfully singing the melody pounding on the earth.

Correcular day.
Living being talking, taking, making, the towering dog sinisterly rising.
Creating chaos.
Burrowing in like a picture in a grave-yard lying on a tombstone.
In the middle of hell it is.
Time has taken.
Time has given.
Time is here.
Time is there.
Traveling wandering, loitering the world beyond reality.
Living time.
Breathing time.
Taking you.
Taking me.
Sound of life.
Sound of death.
Sound of time.

Boundless

The world has died and left me a prisoner.
Lost in an endless forest of spirits.
Seeking love they are.
Bound to realm where love has no meaning.
While search for them selves.
They found it.

The raining plague upon which they dwell.
The reincarnated child of which has no soul.
The bandid house where the wicked are raped and severed of breath.
Being of sin they are.
Jagged and burned by the sow of life.
Read the story.

Joined by hate and greed.
Seeing the last of the wright and truthful.
Landed the angel of one wing.
Held by Satan it was.
Joke and laugh if you must.
But when the body who lays deep beneath.
Floats to the surface.
You shall see the light.

Cherish The Blade

Cherish the blade.
Blade of steel.
Blade of steam.
Blade we made.
Made of chancing column.
Starting rhythm.
Recognizing you and me.
Draping sleep.
Stony lie.
Carpeting prune.
Darning strength.
Bargaining choice.
Chosen as we are.
Candling brew.
Turbular claim.
Marks men tamed.
Collaborate scheme.
Joining life to jade.
Slaying the drooling rabler under tork.
Stumbling lion to be obeyed.
Fundleing terret by the prayed.
Never to be denied.

Cherish the blade.
Blade of steel.
Blade of steam.
Blade we made.
Made of miraculous injunction.
Molded together.
By the pounding of a hammer.
Against the steel on the cold anvil.
Dipping it into water as steam rushes off the glowing smoldering metal.
A sword made for battle.

Galatians

Abandoned hope.
Fallen structure of the eye.
Rugged trade.
Spangled banner up heeled.
Rebel of the legacy.
Changing trickery.
Tackling fever recklessly under marshal law.
Prince of darkness.
Waking injustice of the retched cadocomes.
Dripping institute of crap.
Slicing immoral subliminal mind drain.
There once was something called.
Galatians always on my side.
Galatians always on my side.

Enchanted race left behind.
Gallows up rooted.
Execrators laid to rest.
Punishment uncompleted.
Exhumation of the preglator.
Warping loco.
Blazing monarchy.
Ripping the attacker.
From his train stop.
Turning back on your way.
To the lost civilization.
Known to be extinct.
There once was something called.
Galatians, Galatians always on my side.
Galatians, Galatians always on my side.

GARDEN

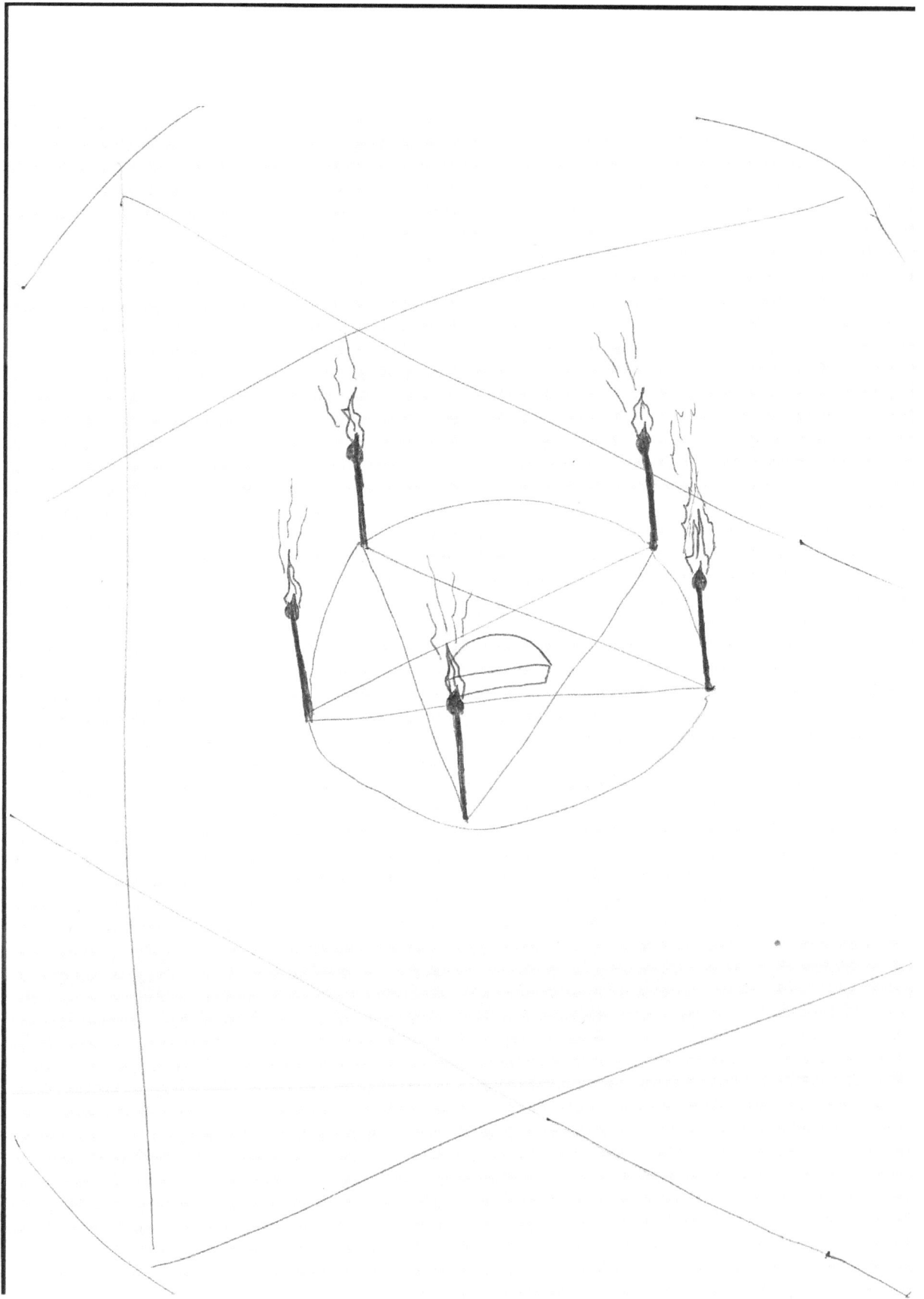

The Remembering

The light is creeping up right behind us.
Their taking all our darkness away.
We got to defend our domain.
Defend the garden.
Defend the garden.
Defend the mighty shadow garden.

The Guardians have brought the light to kill the darkness and take our power away.
We-say take the light back where it came.
Cause were going to fight are way right through all the pain.
We must defend the garden.
Defend the garden.
Defend the mighty shadow garden.

For it's the source of all our power.
And with out it were defenseless.
Against the guardians of light.
It has never been told.
But once there was an equal amount of light and darkness.
Until the one who came from within the darkness.
An seen our people confused and lost to the light.

So he built the shadow garden.
Saving us all.
For we are people of darkness.
Where we don't need no light to follow.
So we built a mighty nation of darkness.
Sending the light away.
Where we lived in peace and loved the darkness.
For the light is evil.
And the guardians declared war upon us.
Now were engaged in battle with our creators.
For they wish to destroy us and the garden.
So defend the garden.
Defend the garden.
Defend the mighty Shadow garden.

Lantrakta

Lantrakta come to me.
Come to the darkness.
Come to the snare.
Where you shall become immortal.
The snare is where you'll get entrapped into the garden.

Lantrakta where have you been.
Staring through the red window spying on the dead.
Watching them standing in line.
Caught between time.
Lantrakta come back to me.
The light is no place to be free in.

Lantrakta the darkness has shown me the way.
Right through all the pain.
Join us or the light will take your soul away.
Lantrakta come to me.
Find your way to the shadow garden, garden, garden.

The Pain

I remember when we had to run from the light.
And hide in caves and creepy hallows.
The children were starving and our people were dying.
For the pain was unbearable.
There was no more day or night just great flashes of light.

Twisted arrangement.
Darken reddish skies.
Dust particles fill the air.
Radioactivity everywhere.
Nuclear destructions been here.

Sasid jonis.
Sabis serious.
Labis larious.
Sonid soronsis.
Salin sarasis.
Sabod sious.
Bashid death by 94r.

Hiding in the darkness.
We learned the world is different then we believe it to be.
We've learned to use pain to build power.
For pain is power and ours to control.

The pain.
The pain.
The pain.
Inevitably we've changed.

Changed to creatures that stalk for prey.
Creatures that come out of the darkness.
To absorb the light.
Inevitably we are creatures of the night.

The immortal flesh.
The immortal flesh.
The immortal flesh.
The immortal flesh.

Rest or Let Live

Ransoble straight.
Canister containing potent soul.
Arriving at maximum level.
To take your mind and give you helplessly evil soul.
Made of burning death.
At the right of marking.
Luxurious rights of life.
Ripped of sound.

Raising pounding closer to your merit of last return.
Coming against the matrix of time.
Do the earthlings see the entrance.
To the amidst of the wastelands.
Where life is returned to consciousness.
Resting at hand.
The light has past and your left in the cold.

Descending to a plain newly found.
Rendering silent beings.
To roam and hounder the earth.
As if it was theirs.
Remaining crescent.
Corrupting the bleeding desert.
To where we shall meet.
Receiving our ensemble.
To the larsing structure.
Being you are the last to be revented.

The Black Light

Wandering you will do.
Yes wandering.
Lost to the light.
Never to feel the power of darkness.
Missing the gate.
Entrapped in a tomb of light.

The gate has opened.
And you've lost your trail.
Wandering you will do.
Yes wandering.
Lost to the light.

Darkness shall prevail.
We shall defeat the light.
And rule for eternity.
In the black light led the dreadest of fears.
The black light has tinted.
Giving us a sign.
A sign that the world is nearing its fate.

For the black light was created by the shadow garden.
And the garden was created to free us.
If it wasn't for the shadow garden.
Wandering you will do.
Yes wandering.
Lost to the light.

The Willing Lie at The Front

Satan calls the willing.

Wandering last wishes.
Deeply stranded in your cold waste land of reality.
Hateful courage.
Souring through the garden above.
Scattered feelings at the ends of time.
Here you are again lost in the light.

Light blasting through the heavens.
Enchanting beings once possessed the earth.
Calmly but surely.
Creeping through boundaries.
The darkness hesitates.
For the movement of the shadow garden.
That lies beyond the great consciousness of the unwilling.

Satan calls the willing.

Willing of mind and soul.
In the flesh shall come the creator of the mighty and righteous shadow garden.
Which will set us free of mortality.
Watching the last front of our mightiest rise.
Eternity is where we lie.
And death awaits the relenting.

Satan calls the willing.

www.ingramcontent.com/pod-product-compliance
Lightning Source LLC
Chambersburg PA
CBHW081159090426
42736CB00017B/3394